'All those
excessive, useless
regrets . . .'

C. P. CAVAFY
Born 1863, Alexandria, Egypt
Died 1933, Alexandria, Egypt

This selection of poetry covers a thirty-six-year
period in Cavafy's life, 1897–1933. Originally written
in Greek, this selection is taken from *The Selected
Poems of Cavafy*, translated by Avi Sharon,
Penguin Classics, 2008.

CAVAFY IN PENGUIN CLASSICS
The Selected Poems of Cavafy

C. P. CAVAFY

Remember, Body . . .

Translated by
Avi Sharon

PENGUIN BOOKS

PENGUIN CLASSICS

UK | USA | Canada | Ireland | Australia
India | New Zealand | South Africa

Penguin Books is part of the Penguin Random House group of companies
whose addresses can be found at global.penguinrandomhouse.com.

Penguin
Random House
UK

This selection published in Penguin Classics 2015
002

Translation copyright © Avi Sharon, 2008

The moral right of the translator has been asserted

Set in 9/12.4 pt Baskerville 10 Pro
Typeset by Jouve (UK), Milton Keynes
Printed in Great Britain by Clays Ltd, St Ives plc

A CIP catalogue record for this book is available from the British Library

ISBN: 978–0–141–39746–7

www.greenpenguin.co.uk

Contents

Desires 1

Candles 2

Dangerous Things 3

Very Seldom 4

Painted Things 5

Morning Sea 6

The Café Entrance 7

One Night 8

Return 9

Far Away 10

He Vows 11

I Left 12

Chandelier 13

Since Nine O'Clock 14

Insight 15

When They Come Alive 16

Pleasure 17

I Have Gazed So Much   18

In The Street   19

The Tobacconist's Window   20

The Passage   21

In the Evening   22

Grey   23

Beside the House   24

The Next Table   25

Remember, Body . . .   26

Days of 1903   27

The Afternoon Sun   28

To Live   29

On the Ship   30

That They May Come   31

Their Beginning   32

In an Old Book   33

In Despair   34

Before Time Could Change Them   35

He Came to Read   36

In the Twenty-fifth Year of His Life 37

The Dreary Village   38

In the Bars   39

Days of 1896   40

Two Young Men, Twenty-three
    to Twenty-four Years Old   41

Days of 1901   43

Days of 1908   44

A Young Writer – in His
    Twenty-fourth Year   46

Picture of a Young Man of
    Twenty-three, Painted by
    His Friend of the Same Age,
    an Amateur   47

Days of 1909, 1910 and 1911   48

Lovely Flowers, White Ones,
    That Matched So Well   49

In the Same Space   51

The Mirror in the Entrance Hall   52

He Asked About the Quality   53

Desires

Like the beautiful bodies of those who died young,
tearfully interred in a grand mausoleum
with roses by their heads and jasmine at their feet –
so seem those desires that have passed
without fulfilment; without a single night
of pleasure, or one of its radiant mornings.

Candles

The days of the future stand before us
like a line of burning candles –
golden candles, warm with life.

Behind them stand the days of our past,
a pitiful row of candles extinguished,
the nearest still sending up their smoke:
cold and melted, withered sticks.

I don't want to look; their image makes me sad,
it saddens me to recall their kindling.
I look ahead at the ones still burning.

I don't want to turn and see, with horror,
how quickly the line of shadow lengthens,
how quickly the number of snuffed candles grows.

Dangerous Things

Myrtias, a Syrian studying in Alexandria
during the reigns of Constans and Constantius,
half pagan and half Christian convert:
'Fortified with contemplation and long study,
I will not fear my passions, like a coward;
I will give my body entirely to pleasure,
to dreamed-of joys, the most brazen
erotic desires, the most depraved passions in my blood,
all without fear. For when I so wish it –
and I *will* so wish it, fortified as I'll be
with contemplation and long study –
at those critical moments I will find again
my ascetic spirit, as pure as it was before.'

Very Seldom

An old man, stooped and spent,
crippled by the years and by excess,
walks slowly across the alley.
But as he enters his house
to hide his wretched state and his old age,
he muses on that share of youth he still claims.

Young boys today recite his verses.
His fancies pass across their waking eyes.
Their healthy, sensuous minds,
their muscular, smooth limbs,
are stirred by his vision of beauty.

Painted Things

I love my work and take pains with it. But today
I find the slow pace of composition discouraging.
The weather has got into me. It just gets darker
and darker. Non-stop wind and rain.
I'd rather watch than write.
I'm looking at this painting now:
it shows a handsome boy lying near a spring,
out of breath from running.
Such a beautiful boy! And such a divine noon
which has taken him and induced him to sleep!
I sit and gaze like this for a long time.
Immersed again in art, I recover from the labour of
     creating it.

Morning Sea

Let me stop right here. Let me, too, have a look at nature:
the morning sea and the cloudless sky,
both a luminous blue, the yellow shore, all of it
beautiful, and in such magnificent light.

Let me stop right here. Let me pretend this is actually
what I'm seeing (I really did see it, when I first stopped)
and not, here too, more of those fantasies of mine,
more of those memories, those voluptuous illusions.

The Café Entrance

Something they said beside me
turned my attention towards the café entrance.
There I saw a beautiful body
that Eros must have fashioned with his boundless skill,
designing with delight the symmetrical limbs,
moulding the tall, sculpted frame,
tenderly drawing the face,
and bestowing, with a touch of his hand,
a feeling on the brow, in the eyes and on the lips.

One Night

The room was shabby and miserable,
tucked above a suspect tavern.
A window opened on to the alley,
narrow and unclean. From the tavern beneath
came the voices of workmen
playing cards and carousing.

There, in that humble, commonplace bed,
I possessed the body of love; I possessed
those sensual, rose-red lips of intoxication –
red lips so intoxicating that even now,
as I write these lines, after so many years
all alone in this house, I am drunk with it again.

Return

Return often and take me,
beloved sensation, return and take me –
when the body's memory awakens,
and old longings pulse again in my blood,
when lips and skin remember,
and hands could almost touch again.

Return often and take me at night,
when lips and skin remember.

Far Away

I would like to speak of this memory . . .
But it has grown dim . . . as if no trace of it remains –
for it lies far off in the first years of my youth.

Skin as if made of jasmine . . .
an August evening – was it August? –
I barely recall the eyes now: they were blue, I think.
Ah yes . . . blue, a sapphire blue.

He Vows

Every now and then   he vows to live a better life.
But when night comes   with her own counsels,
with her promises   and her compromises,
when night   comes with her power
over the body   that seeks and yearns,
he returns, lost,   to the same fatal pleasures.

I Left

I allowed no restraint. I gave in completely and left.
I ran toward pleasures that were half real
and half spun by my own mind.
I ran in the radiant night
and drank down strong wines, the kind
that champions of pleasure drink.

Chandelier

In a small, empty room, nothing
but four walls covered in green fabric,
an elegant chandelier glows, ablaze with light;
and in each of the chandelier's flames
burns an erotic fever, an erotic urge.

The fire raging in the chandelier
fills the tiny room, which shines
with a radiance that is in no way familiar.
And from its heat comes a kind of pleasure
not suited for timid bodies.

Since Nine O'Clock

Half past twelve. The time has passed quickly
since I first lit the lamp at nine o'clock,
and sat down here. I've sat without reading,
without speaking. With whom could I speak,
all alone in this house?

Since nine o'clock when I lit the lamp
a ghostly image of my adolescent body
came to me, reminding me
of closed and scented chambers,
and past pleasures – what brazen pleasures!
It brought before my eyes
streets now unrecognizable,
bars once filled with movement, now closed,
cafés and theatres that once existed.

The vision of my body in its youth
brought sorrowful memories also:
the grieving of my family, separations,
the feelings I had for my own kin, feelings
for the dead, whom I little acknowledged.

Half past twelve; how the time has passed.
Half past twelve; how the years have passed.

Insight

The years of my youth, my sensual adolescence –
how clearly I see their meaning now.

All those excessive, useless regrets . . .

I didn't see the meaning then.

For in the dissolute life of my youth
the plans for my poetry were taking shape;
the boundaries of my art were being drawn.

That's why my regrets were never firm,
and my determination to refrain, to change my ways,
lasted two weeks at most.

When They Come Alive

Try to preserve them, poet,
your visions of love,
however few may stay for you.
Cast them, half hidden, into your verse.
Try to hold on to them, poet,
when they come alive in your mind
at night or in the brightness of noon.

Pleasure

The joy and balm of my life is the memory of those hours
when I found and held pleasure just as I had wished it.
The joy and balm of my life is that I was able to avoid
any sensual gratification that seemed routine.

I Have Gazed So Much

I have gazed so much on beauty
that my eyes overflow with it.

The body's curves. Red lips. Voluptuous limbs.
Hair as if taken from a Greek statue,
always lovely, even if uncombed,
tumbling lightly over the snowy brow:
the Dramatis Personae of love that my poetry
demanded . . . in the nights of my youth,
encountered, secretly, in those nights . . .

In the Street

His face, appealing, a little wan;
his languid eyes a chestnut colour;
twenty-five years old but seeming twenty,
with an artist's sense for clothing –
the colour of the tie, the collar's shape –
aimlessly wandering the street
as if still dazed from the illicit passion,
the quite illicit passion he has just enjoyed.

The Tobacconist's Window

Near the brightly lit window
of a tobacconist's shop, they stood amid a crowd of people.
By chance their gazes met
and hesitantly they half expressed
the illicit longing of their flesh.
Later, after several anxious steps along the pavement –
they smiled and gently nodded.

Then the closed carriage . . .
the sensuous mingling of their bodies;
the hands, the lips coming together.

The Passage

Those things he only timidly imagined as a schoolboy
stand open now, revealed before him.
He goes to parties, stays out all night,
gets swept off his feet. And this is perfectly fitting (for our
       art, that is)
as his blood, young and hot,
is pleasure's prize. Lawless, erotic ecstasy
overcomes his body. And his young limbs
give in. In this way a simple youth
becomes worthy of our regard, and briefly he too
crosses over to the Exalted World of Poetry –
this appealing boy with his blood young and hot.

In the Evening

It would not have lasted long in any case.
Years of experience taught me that. And yet,
it was rather hasty, the way Fate ended it.
The good times were brief.
But how powerful the fragrances;
how wonderful the bed we lay in;
what pleasure we gave our bodies!

An echo from those days of pleasure,
an echo from those days came near,
an ember from our youth's fire;
I took one of his letters
and read it over and over until the light faded.

Melancholic, I stepped out on to the balcony –
I stepped out to change my mood by seeing at least
a little of this city that I love,
a little movement in the streets and in the shops.

Grey

Gazing upon a half-grey opal
I suddenly recalled two beautiful grey eyes
I'd once seen. It must have been twenty years ago . . .

We were lovers for a month.
Then he left; to Smyrna I think,
looking for work, and we never saw each other again.

Their beauty must have dimmed by now – if he's even
        alive – those grey eyes;
that beautiful face has surely gone to ruin.

Memory, keep those eyes just as they were.
And memory, whatever you can salvage of that passion of
        mine,
whatever you can, bring back to me tonight.

Beside the House

Yesterday, strolling in a remote neighbourhood,
I passed beside the house
I had entered when I was just a boy.
It was there that Eros first seized my limbs
with his delicious force.

And yesterday,
as I crossed that same old street, suddenly,
through the enchantment that Eros gives,
it was all made beautiful again . . . the shops, the
      pavements, the stones,
the walls and terraces and windows;
nothing unseemly remained.

And while I stood there, gazing up at the door,
while I stood loitering beside the house,
my entire being exuded
a sensual feeling confined within.

The Next Table

He can't be more than twenty-two.
And yet I'm certain it was at least that many years ago
that I enjoyed the very same body.

This isn't some erotic fantasy.
I've only just come into the casino
and there hasn't been time enough to drink.
I tell you, that's the very same body I once enjoyed.

And if I can't recall precisely where – that means nothing.

Now that he's sitting there at the next table,
I recognize each of his movements – and beneath his
      clothes
I see those beloved, naked limbs again.

Remember, Body . . .

Body, remember not only how deeply you were loved,
not only the many beds where you lay,
but also those desires that flashed
openly in their eyes
or trembled in the voice – and were thwarted
by some chance impediment.
Now that all of them are locked away in the past,
it almost seems as if you surrendered
to even those pre-empted desires – how they flashed,
    remember,
in the eyes of those who looked at you, how they trembled
in the voice for you, remember, body.

Days of 1903

I never found them again – so quickly lost,
the poetic eyes, the pallid face,
seen on the street at nightfall.

I never found them again – possessed entirely by chance,
then given up so easily,
and now so agonizingly longed for.
The poetic eyes, the pallid face,
those lips I never found again.

The Afternoon Sun

This room, how well I know it.
Now they're renting it and the one next door
as commercial space. The whole house is now
offices for brokers, salesmen, entire firms.

Ah, this room, how familiar it is!

Here, near the door, stood the sofa,
a Turkish carpet just before it;
nearby was a shelf with two yellow vases;
on the right – no, facing it – was an armoire with a mirror.
The desk where he wrote stood in the middle,
along with three large, wicker chairs.
Beside the window lay the bed
where we made love so many times.

All of these poor old furnishings must still exist
      somewhere.

Beside the window lay the bed;
the afternoon sunlight reached only half way across it . . .

That afternoon, at four o'clock, we parted,
just for a week . . . alas,
that week became forever.

To Live

It must have been one o'clock in the morning,
or one-thirty.

In a corner of the tavern;
behind the wooden partition.
Except for us, the space entirely empty.
An oil lamp was barely glowing.
The waiter on the night shift lay dozing at the door.

No one could have seen us. Regardless,
we'd reached such a state already,
we were past all thought of caution.

Our clothes half undone now – the few we had on,
with divine July burning.

Gratification of the flesh
between half-opened clothes,
the quick baring of the flesh – the ideal image of it
has travelled across twenty-six years, and now has come
to live in these verses.

On the Ship

It certainly bears some resemblance, this small portrait,
done in pencil.

Hastily drawn right there on the ship's deck
one magical afternoon,
the Ionian Sea all around us.

It bears a resemblance. But I remember him as even more
        handsome,
more sensual, almost painfully so,
which casts his features in a more vivid light.
He seems even more handsome to me
now that my soul calls him back, out of Time.

Out of Time. All of these things are so very old –
the sketch, the ship, that afternoon.

That They May Come

One candle will suffice.　The gentle light it gives
suits the ambience better,　makes the room more alluring
for the Shades of Love,　whenever they may come.

One candle will suffice.　The room tonight
should have very faint light.　For deep in reverie
and suggestiveness –　in the softest light –
I will conjure my visions,　lost in feeling,
so the shades may come,　the Shades of Love.

Their Beginning

The fulfilling of their lawless pleasures
now complete, they rise from the bed
and hurriedly dress without speaking.
They emerge separately, furtively from the house,
and as they walk somewhat uneasily down the street,
it appears they suspect something about them betrays
the sort of bed they fell upon just a moment ago.

But what great profit to the artist's life:
tomorrow, the day after, or years later, he'll write
the powerful lines that had their beginning here.

In an Old Book

In an antique book – about a hundred years old –
I found a watercolour sandwiched amid the pages,
totally forgotten, with no signature.
You could see it was the work of a skilful artist;
it bore the title: 'Representation of Love'.

But it should have been 'love of the most extreme
     voluptuaries'.

For it was clear when you looked at the work
(the intent of the artist was easily grasped)
that the boy in this painting was not intended
for those who love in any healthy way,
who remain within the bounds of what is normally permitted –
his deep, chestnut eyes, the exquisite beauty
of his face, his idealized lips that bring
such pleasure to the beloved's body;
those ideal limbs fashioned for the sort of activity
the current morality would call shameless.

In Despair

He's lost him for good,   and now on the lips
of each new lover   he seeks the lips
of the one he lost;   in every embrace
with each new lover   he tries to believe
that he's giving himself   to the same young man.

He's lost him for good,   as if he'd never existed.
The boy wished – so he said –   he wished to be freed
from the stigma and reproach   of that unhealthy pleasure;
from the stigma and reproach   of that shameful pleasure.
It wasn't too late – he said –   for him to break free.

He's lost him for good,   as if he'd never existed.
Through imagination,   and self-delusion,
he seeks those lips   on the lips of others;
he's trying to feel   that lost love again.

Before Time Could Change Them

They wept horribly   at the separation.
Neither had wished it;   it was circumstance,
the need to earn a living,   where one or the other was
                                            obliged
to go far away –   New York or Canada.
Yet at that point their love   was no longer what it had
                                            been.
Their old attraction   had diminished by degrees;
their old attraction   had diminished a good deal.
But neither desired   to be split apart.
It was circumstance, surely.   Or perhaps Destiny itself
was working now as an artist,   separating them at the
                                            point
when their passion subsided,   before time could change
                                            them;
and each to the other   would remain always as he was:
a handsome young man   of twenty-four.

He Came to Read

He came to read; two or three books
are lying open: history and poetry.
But after just ten minutes of reading
he lets them drop. There on the sofa
he falls asleep. He truly is devoted to reading –
but he is twenty-three years old, and very handsome.
And just this afternoon, Eros surged
within his perfect limbs and on his lips.
Into his beautiful flesh came the heat of passion,
and there was no foolish embarrassment
about the form that pleasure took . . .

In the Twenty-fifth Year of His Life

He goes nightly to the saloon
where they'd met the month before.
He made inquiries, but they could tell him nothing.
From what little they'd said, he knew he'd met up
with an entirely unknown subject:
one of the many suspicious, shadowy
young forms who frequented that spot.
Yet he goes to the tavern every night
and sits there watching the entrance,
doggedly watching the entrance.
Perhaps he'll come. Perhaps tonight he'll come.

For three weeks he repeats the ritual.
His mind grows sick with lust.
Kisses linger on his lips.
Every inch of his flesh is racked by longing.
He feels that body's touch all over.
He longs to embrace him again.

He tries, of course, not to betray his emotions.
But sometimes he is almost beyond caring.
Besides, he is well aware of the risk;
he's made up his mind. It's not improbable that this life he
    leads
will expose him to some ruinous scandal.

The Dreary Village

In the dreary village where he works –
an assistant in one of the commercial establishments,
and quite young – he waits
for two or three months to pass,
for two or three months when business might slow
and he could leave for the city, to plunge straight
into the hurly-burly and amusement there;
in the dreary village where he waits –
he fell into bed tonight in a fit of passion,
all of his youth burning with carnal desire,
all of his beautiful youth in its beautiful intensity.
And in his sleep, pleasure came upon him; in his sleep
he sees and holds those limbs, the flesh he desired . . .

In the Bars

I'm wallowing in the bars   and brothels of Beirut.
I had no desire   to stay in Alexandria.
Tamides has left me   for the Eparch's son,
for a villa on the Nile,   and a mansion in town.
To stay in Alexandria   wouldn't do for me.
I'm wallowing in the bars   and brothels of Beirut.
In base debauchery   I lead a dirty, sordid life.
My one consolation,   like long-lasting beauty,
like a scent that has stayed   lingering on my skin,
is that for two years I had   that most exquisite youth,
Tamides, as my own,   as my very own,
and not for a house   or a villa on the Nile.

Days of 1896

He is utterly disgraced.   An erotic proclivity,
quite forbidden   and widely condemned
(yet congenital nonetheless),   was the cause:
for public opinion   was terribly prudish.
Bit by bit he was deprived   of the little income he had;
then came a loss in status,   and the respect he once
                                commanded.
He was nearing thirty   but had never gone a year
in full employment,   or at least a job he could talk about.
At times he earned   some semblance of a livelihood
by brokering meetings   considered shameful.
He ended up one of those who,   if you were seen with him
often enough, you could be   terribly compromised.

But no, that will not do;   this picture isn't right.
The memory of his beauty   deserves better than this.
There is another point of view,   and seen from that angle
he is quite appealing;   a simple and true
child of Eros who,   without hesitation,
placed far above his honour   and reputation,
the pure pleasure   that his pure flesh could give.

Above his own reputation?   But public opinion,
which was so terribly prudish,   so often got it wrong.

Two Young Men, Twenty-three to Twenty-four Years Old

He'd been sitting at the café since half past ten,
expecting him to appear at any moment.
Midnight came and went, and he still waited.
Soon it would be one thirty; the café
was almost completely empty.
He grew tired of reading the newspapers mechanically.
Of his original three shillings
only one remained: while waiting there
he'd spent the rest on coffee and brandy.
He'd smoked all his cigarettes.
The waiting had exhausted him. Alone
all those hours, insidious thoughts began to rankle
about the wayward life he led.

But when he saw his friend arrive – at once
the fatigue, the boredom, and the dark thoughts all
        vanished.

His friend brought unexpected good news:
he'd won sixty pounds playing cards.

Their handsome faces, their buoyant youth,
the sensuous love they both shared
were refreshed, had come alive and were fortified
by those sixty pounds won at cards.

C. P. Cavafy

Now full of joy and strength, sensuousness and beauty,
they departed – not to the homes of their respectable
        families
(where, after all, they were no longer welcome):
but to a place known only to them, a special
establishment of vice, where they requested
a room with a bed, expensive cocktails, and started to
        drink again.
When the drinks ran dry
and it was nearing four in the morning,
they gave themselves, happy at last, to love.

Days of 1901

This is what was so exceptional about him:
that despite all his profligacy
and his vast experience of love,
despite the fact that his comportment
matched his years perfectly,
there were moments – extremely rare
of course – when he gave the impression
that his flesh had almost never been touched.

The beauty of his twenty-nine years,
a beauty so well tested by pleasure,
could at times make one believe
he was a mere adolescent who – a bit awkwardly –
surrenders his chaste body to love for the very first time.

Days of 1908

That year he found himself out of work,
and so he made a living playing cards
or backgammon, and from whatever he could borrow.

He'd been offered work at a small stationer's
for three pounds a month.
Without a second thought he turned it down.
It wouldn't do. That was no salary for him,
a young man of twenty-five,
with a decent education.

He made – or failed to make – two or three shillings a day.
What else could a youth expect to win at cards
or backgammon in the sort of working-class cafés he
    frequented,
no matter how skilfully he played, or how stupid his
    opponents?
As for the loans, that was even worse.
On rare occasions he got a crown. More often, half.
Sometimes just a shilling.

When he was able to escape the grim, nightly ritual
for a week, or sometimes longer,
he would go and freshen up at the baths, with a morning
    swim.

His clothes were in terrible disrepair.
He wore the same suit all the time,
a faded cinnamon-coloured suit.

Ah, days of summer, nineteen hundred and eight,
your vision of him, for beauty's sake,
omitted that faded cinnamon-coloured suit.

Instead, your vision preserved him
just as he was taking it off, casting away
that unworthy clothing, and the mended underwear,
and he stood completely naked, flawless in his beauty; a
     miracle.
His hair uncombed, tossed back,
his limbs lightly tanned
from those naked mornings at the baths and on the beach.

A Young Writer – in His Twenty-fourth Year

Now, brain, work as hard as you can.
A one-sided passion is wearing him thin.
He's in a state of nervous anxiety.
He kisses that adored face every day,
his hands all over those exquisite limbs.
He never loved before with so intense
a passion, but the happy fulfilment of Eros
is wanting; missing is the satisfaction that comes
when there are two who long with the same intensity.

(But these two are not equally given to their illicit passion.
    It possessed only him in full.)

So he is worn down, his nerves completely frayed.
He's jobless too, which makes matters worse.
He borrows a few pounds here and there,
and with difficulty (sometimes he almost has to beg)
he just about gets by.
He kisses those lips he adores; and upon
that exquisite body – which he now knows
merely tolerates him – he takes his pleasure.
Then he drinks and smokes; drinks and smokes,
and loiters in the coffee shops all day,
tediously lugging his heart-ache for that beauty.
Now, brain, work as hard as you can.

Picture of a Young Man of Twenty-three, Painted by His Friend of the Same Age, an Amateur

He completed the portrait   yesterday afternoon.
Now he scans it carefully: the subject is shown
in a grey jacket, dark grey,   unbuttoned, with no vest
and no tie underneath.   The shirt is pink
and left just open enough   to allow a glance
at his fine-looking chest   and his elegant neck.
The brow, on his right,   is almost completely obscured
by a curl of his hair,   that rich, thick hair
(done in the style   he wore that year).
Throughout the portrait   you see the extreme sensuousness
with which he endowed it,   when he painted the eyes,
when he drew the lips . . .   the mouth, those lips,
created for the fulfilment   of a particular pleasure.

Days of 1909, 1910 and 1911

The son of a put-upon, dirt-poor sailor
(from some island in the Aegean),
he worked as a blacksmith's apprentice. He had rags
for clothes, his pitiful working boots were in tatters,
his hands filthy with rust and oil.

In the evening, when the shop closed,
if there were something he especially wanted,
a necktie with a rather high price-tag,
a necktie to wear on Sundays,
or if he caught a glimpse of a nice blue shirt
in the shop window and hankered after it,
he'd sell his body for a shilling or two.

I wonder if Alexandria, in all its glory, in all the long
        history
of its ancient days, had ever seen a youth more exquisite,
more perfect than this boy – who went utterly to waste.
For, of course, no statue or portrait
was ever made. Stuck there in that grimy blacksmith's
        shop,
worn down by the wrack and strain of work,
and by the working man's rough pleasures, the boy went
        quickly to ruin.

Lovely Flowers, White Ones,
That Matched So Well

He entered the café   they used to frequent together.
It was here that his friend   three months ago had said:
'We haven't a farthing between us.   We're utterly broke.
There's nothing left   but loitering in cheap taverns.
I'm telling you straight,   I can't afford to be with you.
Someone else, you know,   is interested in me now.'
This other had promised him   two suits and a few
silk handkerchiefs.   To get him to come back
he searched everywhere   and found twenty pounds.
For twenty pounds,   his friend returned;
but beyond that, surely,   he returned for their friendship,
for the love they shared,   the deep feeling between them.
The other one had lied,   he was a nasty piece of work;
he'd only placed one suit   on order for him, and that
only grudgingly,   after a thousand requests.

But now he no longer   has any desire for the suit,
he has no desire   for silk handkerchiefs,
or twenty pounds,   or even twenty pence.

They buried him on Sunday,   at ten in the morning.
They buried him on Sunday,   a week ago now.

And on the cheap coffin   he laid some flowers,
lovely flowers, white ones,   that matched so well
his youthful beauty,   his twenty-two years.

C. P. Cavafy

When he went in the evening   to the same café
they used to frequent together –   he happened to find
                                                work;

he still had to earn a living –   that dark café
they used to frequent together   was like a knife in his
                                                heart.

In the Same Space

This setting of houses and cafés, the neighbourhood
where I gaze and where I stroll, for years and years.

I have fashioned you in joy and in sorrow,
through so many happenings, out of so many things.

You've been wholly transformed into feeling, for me.

The Mirror in the Entrance Hall

In the entrance hall of the elegant home
stood a large mirror, very old,
acquired at least eighty years ago.

A handsome youth, a tailor's apprentice
(on Sundays an amateur athlete),
was standing with a package. He handed it
to someone at the door who took it inside;
then he waited for the receipt. The tailor's apprentice
remained alone and waited.
He approached the mirror, gazed at his reflection
and straightened his tie. Five minutes later
they came with the receipt. He took it and left.

But the old mirror that during all the many years
of its existence had looked upon
thousands of objects and faces,
the old mirror was happy now,
filled with the satisfaction that it had received,
if only for a few minutes, beauty in all its perfection.

He Asked About the Quality

From the office where he'd been taken on
to fill a position that was trivial and poorly paid
(eight pounds a month, including bonus) –
he emerged as soon as he'd finished the dreary tasks
that kept him bent over his desk all afternoon.
At seven he came out and began to stroll
slowly down the street. He was handsome
in an interesting way, with the look of a man
who had reached the peak of his sensual potential.
He'd turned twenty-nine a month before.

He dawdled along the street, then down
the shabby alleys that led to his apartment.

As he passed a little shop that sold cheap
imitation goods for workmen,
inside he saw a face, a physique
that urged him on, and in he walked,
inquiring about some coloured handkerchiefs.

He asked about the quality of the handkerchiefs
and what they cost; his voice
breaking, almost stifled by desire.
The answers came back in the same tone,
distracted, the low timbre
suggesting veiled consent.

They went on talking about the merchandise –
but their sole aim was for their hands to touch

53

over the handkerchiefs, for their faces,
their lips, as if by chance, to brush against each other:
for some momentary contact of the flesh.

Swiftly and in secret, so that the shop owner,
seated at the back, would never notice.

1. BOCCACCIO · *Mrs Rosie and the Priest*
2. GERARD MANLEY HOPKINS · *As kingfishers catch fire*
3. *The Saga of Gunnlaug Serpent-tongue*
4. THOMAS DE QUINCEY · *On Murder Considered as One of the Fine Arts*
5. FRIEDRICH NIETZSCHE · *Aphorisms on Love and Hate*
6. JOHN RUSKIN · *Traffic*
7. PU SONGLING · *Wailing Ghosts*
8. JONATHAN SWIFT · *A Modest Proposal*
9. *Three Tang Dynasty Poets*
10. WALT WHITMAN · *On the Beach at Night Alone*
11. KENKŌ · *A Cup of Sake Beneath the Cherry Trees*
12. BALTASAR GRACIÁN · *How to Use Your Enemies*
13. JOHN KEATS · *The Eve of St Agnes*
14. THOMAS HARDY · *Woman much missed*
15. GUY DE MAUPASSANT · *Femme Fatale*
16. MARCO POLO · *Travels in the Land of Serpents and Pearls*
17. SUETONIUS · *Caligula*
18. APOLLONIUS OF RHODES · *Jason and Medea*
19. ROBERT LOUIS STEVENSON · *Olalla*
20. KARL MARX AND FRIEDRICH ENGELS · *The Communist Manifesto*
21. PETRONIUS · *Trimalchio's Feast*
22. JOHANN PETER HEBEL · *How a Ghastly Story Was Brought to Light by a Common or Garden Butcher's Dog*
23. HANS CHRISTIAN ANDERSEN · *The Tinder Box*
24. RUDYARD KIPLING · *The Gate of the Hundred Sorrows*
25. DANTE · *Circles of Hell*
26. HENRY MAYHEW · *Of Street Piemen*
27. HAFEZ · *The nightingales are drunk*
28. GEOFFREY CHAUCER · *The Wife of Bath*
29. MICHEL DE MONTAIGNE · *How We Weep and Laugh at the Same Thing*
30. THOMAS NASHE · *The Terrors of the Night*
31. EDGAR ALLAN POE · *The Tell-Tale Heart*
32. MARY KINGSLEY · *A Hippo Banquet*
33. JANE AUSTEN · *The Beautifull Cassandra*
34. ANTON CHEKHOV · *Gooseberries*
35. SAMUEL TAYLOR COLERIDGE · *Well, they are gone, and here must I remain*
36. JOHANN WOLFGANG VON GOETHE · *Sketchy, Doubtful, Incomplete Jottings*
37. CHARLES DICKENS · *The Great Winglebury Duel*
38. HERMAN MELVILLE · *The Maldive Shark*
39. ELIZABETH GASKELL · *The Old Nurse's Story*
40. NIKOLAY LESKOV · *The Steel Flea*

41. HONORÉ DE BALZAC · *The Atheist's Mass*
42. CHARLOTTE PERKINS GILMAN · *The Yellow Wall-Paper*
43. C.P. CAVAFY · *Remember, Body . . .*
44. FYODOR DOSTOEVSKY · *The Meek One*
45. GUSTAVE FLAUBERT · *A Simple Heart*
46. NIKOLAI GOGOL · *The Nose*
47. SAMUEL PEPYS · *The Great Fire of London*
48. EDITH WHARTON · *The Reckoning*
49. HENRY JAMES · *The Figure in the Carpet*
50. WILFRED OWEN · *Anthem For Doomed Youth*
51. WOLFGANG AMADEUS MOZART · *My Dearest Father*
52. PLATO · *Socrates' Defence*
53. CHRISTINA ROSSETTI · *Goblin Market*
54. *Sindbad the Sailor*
55. SOPHOCLES · *Antigone*
56. RYŪNOSUKE AKUTAGAWA · *The Life of a Stupid Man*
57. LEO TOLSTOY · *How Much Land Does A Man Need?*
58. GIORGIO VASARI · *Leonardo da Vinci*
59. OSCAR WILDE · *Lord Arthur Savile's Crime*
60. SHEN FU · *The Old Man of the Moon*
61. AESOP · *The Dolphins, the Whales and the Gudgeon*
62. MATSUO BASHŌ · *Lips too Chilled*
63. EMILY BRONTË · *The Night is Darkening Round Me*
64. JOSEPH CONRAD · *To-morrow*
65. RICHARD HAKLUYT · *The Voyage of Sir Francis Drake Around the Whole Globe*
66. KATE CHOPIN · *A Pair of Silk Stockings*
67. CHARLES DARWIN · *It was snowing butterflies*
68. BROTHERS GRIMM · *The Robber Bridegroom*
69. CATULLUS · *I Hate and I Love*
70. HOMER · *Circe and the Cyclops*
71. D. H. LAWRENCE · *Il Duro*
72. KATHERINE MANSFIELD · *Miss Brill*
73. OVID · *The Fall of Icarus*
74. SAPPHO · *Come Close*
75. IVAN TURGENEV · *Kasyan from the Beautiful Lands*
76. VIRGIL · *O Cruel Alexis*
77. H. G. WELLS · *A Slip under the Microscope*
78. HERODOTUS · *The Madness of Cambyses*
79. *Speaking of Siva*
80. *The Dhammapada*